AUTUMN ON THE FARM

Peggy Heeks
and Ralph Whitlock

Illustrated by Anne Howard

Other books in this series

BUILDINGS ON THE FARM
DAIRY COWS ON THE FARM
PIGS ON THE FARM
POTATOES ON THE FARM
POULTRY ON THE FARM
SHEEP ON THE FARM
SPRING ON THE FARM
SUMMER ON THE FARM
TRACTORS ON THE FARM
WHEAT ON THE FARM
WINTER ON THE FARM

First published in 1985 by
Wayland (Publishers) Ltd
49 Lansdowne Place, Hove
East Sussex BN3 1HF, England

ISBN 0 85078 531 6

Filmset by
Latimer Trend & Company Ltd, Plymouth
Printed in Italy by
G. Canale & C.S.p.A., Turin
Bound in the UK by The Pitman Press, Bath

Contents

In autumn the weather begins to get colder
after the warm summer months.
Leaves fall from the trees and cover the ground.
Many crops which have been growing through
the summer are harvested in autumn.
The farmer has to gather in the crops
before the bad weather spoils them.
He has to store up food for the animals to eat
later in the year.
He is busy preparing for the cold winter months.

Maize is one of the crops which ripen in autumn.
The maize plants are taller than people.
The combine harvester needs special blades
to cut the thick maize stems.
Maize is grown for people and animals to eat.
We eat it as sweetcorn, cornflakes and popcorn.

Apples, pears and plums are ripe in the autumn.
The people in the picture are picking apples
and putting them into crates.
On some fruit farms machines are used to shake
the apples from the trees.
Other machines pick up the apples from the grass.
The farmer sells some of his apples to the shops.
He stores the rest and uses them in the winter.

Grapes are harvested in the autumn.

The grapes are cut off the vines in bunches.

The workers have to be careful
not to damage the soft fruit.

Some grapes are sent to the shops to be sold.

Others are used for making wine or grape juice.

The juice is squeezed out in a big machine
called a press.

At harvest time food shops and supermarkets are
full of good things which the farmers have grown.
In the picture you can see sweetcorn, tomatoes,
runner beans and Brussels sprouts.
There are also pears, plums, blackberries, grapes,
apples to cook and apples to eat raw.

When the harvest is over there are celebrations.
The farm workers and their families
are pleased if the harvest has been good.

Fruit trees need to be looked after carefully.
After the fruit has been picked
the farmer usually prunes each tree.
He cuts off branches that are damaged or dead.
He also cuts the new shoots that grew in summer
to half their length.
He makes each tree a neat shape.
The cuts are disinfected to keep out germs.
Pruning helps the trees
to produce more fruit next year.

In autumn the farmer has to store up food
for his animals to eat in winter.
The barn in the picture is stacked high
with bales of hay for the cows to eat.
There are also bales of straw
for the cows' winter bedding.
The tractor is carrying mangolds
for the cows and sheep to eat when
there is no fresh grass.
There is also some silage outside the barn.

The farmer likes his cows to feed outdoors
for as long as possible in autumn.
He grows leafy crops such as kale and clover
for them to eat when the grass stops growing.
These cows are feeding in a field of clover.
As the nights grow colder the cows
come into covered yards to sleep.

19

Female sheep are called ewes
and male sheep are called rams.
If a farmer wants his ewes to have lambs in spring
he brings a ram to the farm to mate with the ewes.
In the picture the farmer is gathering
the ewes together to check that they are healthy
before they are mated.

Free-range hens find plenty to eat
in the fields in autumn.
They feed on the grain and seed
left behind after the harvest.
At night they sleep in wooden houses.
When the weather gets colder
the hens are moved to the farmyard.
In the farmyard the hens are sheltered
from the autumn storms.

The farmer is busy ploughing the fields in autumn.
The plough turns over the soil and buries
the stubble left behind after the harvest.
When the ploughing is finished
the soil looks brown and shiny.
When you see a field with lines of neat furrows
you know it has just been ploughed.
Some fields are sown with grain in the autumn.
Others are left ready for planting in the spring.

25

When the stubble and weeds are buried
in the ground by the plough
they rot and become part of the soil.
They help make the food that new plants need.
Animal dung also helps to feed new plants.
The picture shows a machine spreading
rotting straw and dung over a field.
Now the soil will have plenty of goodness in it
to feed the new plants.

Once a week the farmer goes to the market
in the nearest town.
All kinds of farm animals
are bought and sold there.
They are taken to and from the market
in big lorries.
The farmer in the picture has just bought
a cow for his dairy herd.

29

On wet days the farm workers
cannot work outdoors in the fields.
They have to find jobs to do indoors.
In autumn the farm machines have to be repaired
and cleaned after the harvest.
These men are making sure that
the combine harvester works properly.
Then it will be ready to use again next year.

Glossary

Autumn   The time between the warm summer
months and the cold winter months.
In the northern countries of the world
autumn is in September, October and November.
In the southern countries of the world
autumn is in March, April and May.

Bale   A bundle of straw or hay tied up
with wire or string.

Combine harvester   A machine which cuts grain crops
in the fields and separates the grain from the stalks.

Disinfectant   Something which kills germs.

Free-range hens   Hens that are kept
in natural surroundings, not in cages.

Furrows   The straight, narrow ditches
made in the ground by a plough.

Mangold   A root crop grown to feed cattle and sheep
in winter. Mangolds are like beetroots.

Pruning   Cutting off the unwanted shoots
from trees and bushes.

Silage   Animal food made from freshly cut grass.

Stubble   The cut stalks of grain crops
left sticking out of the ground after the harvest.

Index

Acknowledgements
The publishers would like to thank *Farmers Weekly*, Grower Publications and the National Farmers Union for supplying reference material for the illustrations in this book.